"Mr. Best, will you get down our pads?" said Ben.

"We'll make frogs," said Maggie.

"I'll make big ones," said Robbie.

"How your frogs look is up to you," said Mr. Best.

1

"Mr. Best, look at my frog!" said Ben.

"Mr. Best, look at MY frog!" said Maggie.

Mr. Best went over to see their frogs.

Then he said, "They look a lot like the
frogs that we see on our walks.
Great frogs!"

"Mr. Best, look at my frogs!" said Robbie.

"Great frogs!" said Mr. Best.

"Frogs can't be red!" said Ben.

"Where did you see red frogs?" said Maggie.

"MY frogs can be red," said Robbie.

"I like red, so I made red frogs."

"Mr. Best, can all of us make red frogs —
big frogs — frogs with SPOTS,
if we want to?" said Maggie.

"How your frogs look is up to you,"
said Mr. Best.
"So you can."

And so they did.

"Great frogs!" said Mr. Best.